TALKING BONES: a play

by Shay Youngblood

Blue Cloud Press

www.shayyoungblood.com

Book cover design by Jessie Glass

ISBN -13: 978-1482642230
ISBN -10: 1482642239

For Carrie Bessie Ross (1910-1993), Lillian Kemp and the spirits of the ancestors who whisper in my ear

Acknowledgments
The author is grateful for the guidance, support and invaluable dramaturgical advice of Anna Deveare-Smith, Mame Hunt, Sydné Mahone, Aishah Rahman, Paula Vogel and the Brown University Graduate Playwriting Workshop and NewPlays acting ensemble. Special thanks to Laura Pirott-Quintero, Daniel Alexander Jones, Kate Rushin, Pat Powell and the Saints: Marge Salvodon and Teresa Langle. For a place in their hearts and a room of my own; Yaddo, McDowell Colony, and Blue Mountain Center. Aché

Authors Note

I grew up in a house where the elders heard voices and it was understood that these voices were the voices of the ancestors. I didn't think it odd until I went out into the world and learned that 'people who hear voices are crazy'. I felt like I was straddling both of those worlds. So I started writing this play about women who hear voices, how these three women respond to their inner voices, and how they respond to the ancestors.

Talking Bones is set in Ancestor's Books & Breakfast, a half empty bookstore in a small Southern town, where three generations of women, Ruth, her daughter Baybay and her grand-daughter Eila, hear the ancestors through a broken hearing aid, whispers in the dark and in talking bones. The ancestors bring a message about love, faith and family. Ruth, the matriarch, needs to settle her affairs before she dies. She interprets the voices she hears as those of the ancestors guiding her. Baybay wants to be free of her mother's traditions. Eila, tries to build a bridge between the two women while creating a place for new rituals and new beginnings. It's a complex journey for all but in the end, the ancestors can be heard whispering – joyous and hopeful.

Shay Youngblood, 2013

There are those of us who straddle.
We are born in one place…sent to
achieve in the larger culture, and in
order to survive we work out a way
to be who we are in both places…
-Bernice Johnson Reagon

…our mouths utter obscure prophesies.
our minds are invaded by images of the future.
we are the strange ones, with half our beings
always in the spirit world…
-Ben Okri, *The Famished Road*

Sometimes I hear a voice in my soul, we are one it says.
-*He and I*

TALKING BONES premiered at the Penumbra Theatre Company, St. Paul, Minnesota, January 26 through February 20, 1994 with the following cast:

BAYBAY Laurie Carlos

MR. FINE Lou Bellamy

OZ Daniel Alexander Jones

RUTH Kathryn Gagnon

EILA Amy Monique Waddell

Directed by Robbie McCauley

Produced by Lou Bellamy

Scenic Designer Seitu K. Jones

Choreographer Marlies Yearby

Lighting Designer Mike Wangen

Sound Designer John Sims, Jr.

Composer Olu Dara

Properties Designer Dean Coke

Stage Manager Scott Peters

Costume Designer Deidrea Whitlock

CHARACTER NOTES

EILA (pronounced Eye-lah): Daughter of Baybay, in her early twenties. Looking for answers to control visions and voices in her head, and someone to accompany her on her mission to build a bridge of understanding between two worlds.

BAYBAY: Daughter of Ruth. Glamorous wanna be-artist in her early forties, slightly out of step. Looking for a way out of a life trapped taking care of her mother. Often ignores or misinterprets the voices she hears.

RUTH: Mother of Baybay, Grandmother of Eila. Dignified, aristocratic woman in her early sixties. Trying to settle her affairs and family business before she dies. Hears voices through her hearing aid.

OZ: Young man in his mid to late twenties. Hip, homeless and usually moving to some inner hip-hop beat, he is looking for a place to belong.

MR. FINE: A businessman in his forties. A seductive, idea man who feels his chance at success rests with Baybay and the café she runs.

COSTUMES
Although the setting and theme have a surreal quality the characters' dress is contemporary/everyday. EILA wears a simple, lime-green, black polka dot (kiwi) dress or blouse with black tights and dark flat shoes or black combat boots.
BAYBAY's attire is glamorous, slightly tacky, and sexually suggestive. RUTH wears a light, neutral-colored flowing dress. OZ wears a dark knit cap, loose, comfortable clothes and although he is homeless, he has a neat appearance. MR. FINE wears an elegant, double-breasted suit.

TALKING BONES
A play for three women and two men

CHARACTERS

EILA daughter of Baybay, in her early 20s

BAYBAY daughter of Ruth, early 40s

RUTH mother of Baybay, early 60s

OZ homeless man, mid to late 20s

MR. FINE a businessman, 40s

TIME: The present. Winter.

PLACE: Ancestor's Books & Breakfast, a half empty bookstore in a small southern town.

Playing time: 90 minutes.

Set: Simple, two playing areas.

The Story: Set in the Ancestor's Books & Breakfast, the ancestors play a major role in daily activity. Ruth, Baybay and Eila can hear them through a broken hearing aid, a whisper and in talking bones. The ancestors bring a message about love, faith and family.

TALKING BONES
a play by Shay Youngblood

SCENE ONE: *Ancestor's Books & Breakfast. Hundred of books are piled on the floor and scattered all around the room. Oversized, brightly-colored books hang from the ceiling and branches of a large tree growing inside the café and sit on the half-empty bookshelves. A café table for customers hosts brightly-decorated chairs. Afrocentric posters of Africa and African-American heroes decorate the walls and hang in the air. Three small altars with flowers, a candle and other objects are placed in separate corners.*

AT RISE: *MR. FINE is seen through the window giving a bunch of flowers to OZ along with elaborate instructions. Inside the café BAYBAY is wearing a glamorous (leopard-print or satin) bathrobe. She begins waltzing around the room enraptured in "movie music" (theme music in the genre of epic films). After a few moments, she becomes depressed, leans on the counter in blue light watching a film the audience can't see. The window becomes a movie screen.*

BAYBAY. My life until today has been merely an audition for the real thing. *(Pause.)* When is it gonna be my turn? *(BAYBAY walks around the room talking to herself, but someone is listening. She sips on a diet soda as she occasionally puts books in empty boxes. She answers unseen voices.)* Say what? What's my problem? I'm thirty-five years old...Okay, so I'm forty. How did I get here? Where did I turn left when I should've turned right? I followed every direction in the book, and this is where? This can't be my life! Can't be. My life was supposed to have more meaning, go slower, be...be better than this. *(Angry.)* I've given away almost every one of these damn books. I have poured my last cup of wisdom tea and stirred my last pot of backbone soup. Forty years is a long-ass wait. Do you hear me, whose ever turn it is to listen? It's a long time to wait! *(Pause.)* What I need to stay here for? *(Pause to listen.)* Hush. You hear me? Don't you tell her nothing. Shhh. Shhh. Shhh. Now you listen to me...

(OZ watches BAYBAY through the window. He drinks in the smell of the flowers, eats a flower petal then enters the shop.)

OZ *(whispering).* Lady, these flowers...

BAYBAY. You don't have to whisper, she can't hear you.

OZ. Who can't hear me?

BAYBAY *(flips on the lights).* The old lady. She can't hear you. Her hearing aid is busted. That thing cost me a fortune. The witch probably broke it herself. It's hooked up to her deaf side, you know, but it sends signals to her good ear. It's like a transistor.

OZ. Some old lady's got a radio in her ear?

BAYBAY. What you got there?

OZ. Flowers...

BAYBAY. For the dead! Why you bring me these half-dead flowers!

OZ. They taste pretty fresh.

BAYBAY. They'll be dead in a few days and what am I supposed to do with some more half-dead things. And stop whispering, this is not a funeral home. I told you she can't hear you. Her hearing aid is messed up. What do they call you?

OZ. Osborn, m'am. My name is Osborn.

BAYBAY. I didn't ask your name. And I ain't no ma'am. I ask what they call you?

OZ. Oz. Home folks call me Oz. Lady, these flowers, where do you want me to put them?

BAYBAY. (*dramatic*) Flowers ain't what I need.

OZ. I don't know nothing about what you need, lady. I'm delivering flowers today. Why don't you read the card. There's a card here.

RUTH *(yells from offstage).* Baybay, who's out there?

BAYBAY. Go back to bed.

RUTH. Who's out there, I said? She back yet?

BAYBAY. It's a delivery.

RUTH. What? I say she back yet?

BAYBAY *(shouts)*. Delivery. *(Mouths.)* Shit.

RUTH. What you doing out there? Who's out there? They told me strangers were coming. People I ain't never seen before. The ancestors said it plain. Any strangers out there?

(RUTH enters wheeling herself in her wheelchair. A large white umbrella lies across her lap. Her apron pocket holds bones wrapped in African fabric. She rolls over to OZ, eyeing him, circling him.)

RUTH. You a stranger?

OZ. You ever seen me before?

RUTH. Could be I seen you in a dream...Boy, you got a question?

OZ. In this dream you had, was I delivering flowers? See, I got these flowers...*(Offers them to RUTH.)*

RUTH. You better get them things outta my face. I ain't dead yet. Cut flowers make offerings for the ancestors, when you need to ask for things like good health, love or money. Looks like I'm gonna need my umbrella soon but don't be giving me no flowers today.

BAYBAY. You ain't gonna need that umbrella for a long time.

(RUTH throws the bones, listens, then picks them up.)

NOTE: Throwing the bones may be mimed using a sound cue for effect.

OZ. The paper didn't say nothing about rain today. I got the weather report here in my right shoe and I'm reading sunny with a chance of rainbows. Lady, what you doing with them bones? *(RUTH ignores him.)* What kind of bones you got there? Them neck bones? I like neck bones.

EILA'S VOICE. On the continent of Africa, in the days of old, the griots kept our stories in the marrow of their souls. In ancient times the griots were buried in the hollow of the baobab tree. And two thousand seasons passed. And the baobab trees were cut down like angry splinters and the bones of the griots spilled onto the ground. Talking bones, talking bones, talking bones...

OZ. Who said that?

RUTH. The bones say you been dreaming under the moon. Say you hungry. You come to the right place.

BAYBAY. Mama, be nice. Go back to bed.

RUTH *(mocking BAYBAY)*. Mama, be nice. Go back to bed. *(Beat.)* I ain't sick, I ain't dead and I ain't your mama. Mother Dear. Can you do something right just once? I've asked you to call me Mother Dear.

OZ. Lady, where do you want me to put these flowers?

RUTH. That ain't a proper question.

BAYBAY. I don't care where you put them. All these years and here come some flowers gonna be dead in two days. This ain't enough.

RUTH. What the hell you think you deserve, a medal?

BAYBAY. Don't start with me this evening, Mama.

OZ. The sign outside say you serve books with breakfast. You got food in here?

BAYBAY *(preachy, quoting)*. "Knowledge is the cornerstone of life. They said serve them and you also will be served." We serve books by and about African Americans and other cultures of color for the nourishment of the mind, body and spirit. *(BAYBAY picks up a book at random and begins reading from it.)* "Africans did not suffer cultural amnesia when they stepped off the slave ships...

BAYBAY. Southern planters selected Africans for importation to North America on the basis of their skills in agriculture, medicine, carpentry, and so on...The Africans' unpaid labor made slavery efficient and economical....Although white slavers are long dead, their children and the U.S. economy continue to benefit from the interest on the profits of slavery through institutional racism"... *(She stops reading)* and collective amnesia about that forty acres and a mule. What am I supposed to do with all this information? Call 411 and give it to them? I want to star in my own movie.

RUTH. You learned everything books could teach you and you still don't have no common sense. *(RUTH cocks her head and taps on her ear to better hear the Ancestors.)* Now what you want? No, I don't know who he is. Boy, what they call you?

OZ. Oz. Home folks call me Oz.

RUTH. He say home folks, whoever they is, call him Oz. Huh? *(Pauses to listen.)* Boy, you must be one of the strangers.

OZ. If anybody will take them I'm delivering these flowers. If you don't want them I'll eat them.

RUTH. Say he deliver flowers. He gonna eat them. *(Listening.)* If you can hear him answer, why don't you ask him yourself and leave me alone.

BAYBAY. You listening to them voices again, Mama? Why don't you listen to me?

RUTH. You ain't talking about nothing. They the ones want to know about this boy. I ain't interested. *(Pause.)* Where them flowers come from? Ain't nobody dead yet.

OZ. Lady, I have to go.

RUTH. They say they want to talk to him.

BAYBAY. Mama!

(BAYBAY, resigned to obeying her mother, goes to stand by the door. She picks up a book and points it at OZ.)

OZ. Look, lady, I ain't had a meal in two days. All I want is something good to eat. Tell me what you need, I'll go get it for you.

(OZ's feet are frozen to the spot where he stands.)

BAYBAY. Now what you want me to do with him? They tell you that?

RUTH. Be quiet so I can hear. *(listening)*

(OZ tries desperately to move but his feet are heavy to the floor as if he is standing in quicksand)

OZ. If I don't get back soon I'll lose my spot at the bus station. It starts getting crowded around this time.

BAYBAY. You gonna lose your life if you don't shut up. *(BAYBAY whispers to the Ancestors.)* Shhh. Shhh. Shhh. Talk to Mama, I ain't listening. *(To OZ.)* Be still, you making me nervous.

RUTH. What's your favorite color, boy?

OZ. Kiwi.

BAYBAY. What kind of color is that?

OZ. It's a fruit, the inside of a fruit. The meat is green. The seeds are black.

RUTH. What size shoe you wear?

OZ. Twelve and a half double D.

BAYBAY. Your mama must've had a seizure when them boats sailed out.

RUTH. Baybay, if I have to tell you to shut up one more time I'm gonna open this umbrella and take you with me.

(RUTH shakes her umbrella menacingly at BAYBAY.)

RUTH. Boy, what is your mother's maiden name?

OZ. Leveaux. Mama was a mojo scientist. What's that got to do with...

RUTH. Boy, don't play with me! You ever had a sex disease? *(Pause.)* Well, answer me.

OZ *(embarrassed)*. No!

RUTH. No, what?

OZ. No, ma'am. I've had a lot of things but I never had a sex disease.

(RUTH throws the bones, listens. OZ's feet are freed.)

RUTH. What you plan on doing with your life?

OZ. I used to be a poet. This was my signature poem. *(Recites with movement.)* "I lived in a house with a window. The house burned down to the ground but the window waits. Where there is a window, there is still hope."

RUTH. So you're a messenger.

BAYBAY. That ain't no job.

RUTH. Let me do this.

(OZ's music. Hip-hop style. OZ raps in lighting effect)

OZ. I want to be a engineer, a architect, a writer, a fighter, a wrong to righter. A rapper, a tapper, a two-fisted zapper. Put out the fire, wake up the man. My mama said I could go far. I could dance, all the way to France. One foot forward, two steps back, step on the line, break your daddy's back. Through my feet the sages speak.

(OZ does a variety of hip-hop and African dance steps wildly around the room. At the end of the music he is exhausted.)

BAYBAY. So they speak through your big old feet.

(OZ's feet are frozen in place again.)

RUTH. Baybay, I said hush. I can't hardly hear for your mouth. They asking about your life, boy. What you gonna do with it?

OZ. There's a lot of things I want to do. I got cravings.

BAYBAY. You pregnant, flower boy?

RUTH. Hush! I got a granddaughter I need to get settled before they come get me. They said strangers were coming.

(RUTH points her umbrella skyward.)

BAYBAY. They not coming to get you tomorrow, Mama! This boy still guessing about his future and you trying to give my baby to him. He can't even dance.

RUTH. Eila's coming back because it's the right thing to do. She never should have left here. You the one pushed her out there like you know so much. When you mess with fire you liable to get barbecued.

BAYBAY. I went to the city and I didn't fall through the cracks.

RUTH. Then why you come back?

BAYBAY. You know good and well why, to take care of you.

RUTH. You just as tied to this place as I am, and so is Eila. She's just like you and me, she needs the power in this place.

BAYBAY. I'm plugging up my ears and putting on my travelling shoes.

RUTH. Give me another good reason to snatch that hair off your head and crack you like a coconut. We're special. We can hear them…

OZ. You hear music too?

RUTH. The music is there if you'd just listen. You want to dance, you got to listen to the beat. Listen! You hear that?

(OZ listens intently. Pause. There is a loud knocking at the front door. EILA's music: Jazz/Mellow Rhythm and Blues.)

EILA *(offstage)*. Mama? Grammie? You in there?

RUTH. Now who else gonna be in here?

BAYBAY. Eila? Is that you, baby?

EILA *(offstage)*. Yeah, Ma. Open up.

(BAYBAY opens the door. EILA enters wearing green with black sequins . She carries an open, yellow umbrella. EILA listens to the music trying to figure out where it's coming from. OZ stares at EILA in amazement as if he sees a beautiful apparition.)

EILA. Nice rhythms.

RUTH. Don't bring that open umbrella in here.

BAYBAY. Sugar, I'm glad you're back. Did you miss me, honey?

(EILA looks at BAYBAY but does not respond.)

RUTH. She sure didn't come back here for the pleasure of your company. I can see it in her eyes. She can see things, feel them too, can't you, granddaughter?

EILA. In my bones.I got scratches on my bones.

BAYBAY. Didn't you have a good time? I told you to go to botanical gardens and dance halls and sidewalk cafés.

EILA. I was looking for something.

(EILA makes eye contact with OZ.)

OZ. You're wearing kiwi!
EILA. Searching for somebody.

OZ. Somebody.

EILA. To walk with me, listening to the wind.

OZ. Wind.

EILA. I lived inside my head, between the pages of books.

OZ. "Ah, that I were dark and nightly! How I would suck at the breasts of light."

EILA. "Oh, but I am a forest, and a night of dark trees: but he who is not afraid of my darkness, will find banks full of roses under my cypresses."

EILA & OZ. Nietzsche." *

* *Nietzsche, Friedrich Wilhelm (1844-1900) was a German philosopher.*

OZ. I dreamed about you.

BAYBAY. Keep your empty mind off my daughter.

RUTH. Them New York City sidewalks ain't as exciting as you thought? Too many cracks to slip through. Don't think you gonna come back here and worry me. I was just getting used to you being gone.

EILA. They called me home. (EILA kisses a reluctant RUTH. To OZ) Who are you?

OZ. I've been trying to deliver these flowers but something's got a hold on me...

EILA. They're so pretty.

OZ. You taste like yellow flowers.

EILA. I remember you. I remember you. Your eyes said hope. In the dream your eyes had lips, they said hope.

OZ. I'm afraid I'll lose my place at the bus station. It gets cold if I have to sleep in a stall. It stinks in there and sometimes they turn the lights out. Even Nietzsche can't give me comfort in there.

EILA. Grammie! You holding him here?

RUTH. Don't you Grammie me. How many times I got to tell you, call me Grandmother Dear. I'm not holding nobody, nowhere.

EILA. What's your name?

OZ. Home folks call me Oz. Call me Oz. Can you help me?

BAYBAY. Says he guess he wants to be a dancer.

RUTH. What you wanna dance?

OZ. Excuse me?

EILA. What kind of dancing you wanna do?

OZ. Dance of life. *(Dances a few steps.)*

BAYBAY. What do you know about life? I'm the one who's got something to dance about. I've lived enough to have books written about me, movies made to glorify my name, songs sung to praise my struggle to survive raising a stubborn child and caring for an ungrateful mother. My freedom is coming in a little while and I'm gonna have my second chance.

(EILA has found the card on the flowers.)

EILA. Mama, do you know who these flowers are from?

BAYBAY. I ain't thinking about them flowers.

EILA. They're from somebody named Mr. Fine.

BAYBAY. Mr. Fine! These flowers are from him? He's the gentleman made an offer on the store. He wants to redecorate, turn it into a classy nightclub for celebrity types.

RUTH. You think platform shoes gonna be disco dancing on my grave? Think again. This is my home. And what about the ancestors, who's gonna honor the bones? Who's gonna call out the names if we're gone?

EILA. Mama, you know you can't sell this place.

BAYBAY. I'm a flesh and blood, grown woman. I don't have to answer to nobody in this room or outside of it. Look around here. The last time we had a customer was three days ago and that was Mattie's lil boy looking for *Soul on Ice.* He wanted to know when the next revolution was gonna be. Ain't much left in here but dreams. I don't want to wake up and still be in this dream. I'm living, Mama, in spite of you.

(BAYBAY exits.)

RUTH. And they thought I was crazy. *(Yelling after BAYBAY.)* You can't get away from them that easy. What would happen to your soul if we left this place? Who would make the offerings? Bones are buried here, people you know. She don't make a teaspoonful of sense. *(Beat.)* I'm not gonna be able to hear you much longer. You got to honor the bones. You got to call out people's names.
(RUTH taps on her hearing aid to better hear the Ancestors. To OZ.) They want to see some.

EILA. What, Grammie?

RUTH. They want to see his life dancing.

EILA. I'd like to see it too, Oz.

OZ *(feet released, he begins walking backwards, testing his freedom).* There's a couple of things I need to take care of out there. I'm so hungry.

EILA. I can feed you.

(OZ dances as he speaks. OZ's music. He moves as if the rhythm of life pulses through his body, as if he is possessed by spirit.)

OZ. These hands have felt the hard side of life, touched the soft side of living. Look at my skin, what do you see? Flesh and blood or just a heartbeat. Hot breath. Dream. Waking desire. My eyes open in the morning. I get up looking for right, turning left, keeping my face forward, my chin up. Life is what you make happen between the beginning and the end in spite of the odds against you. Life is looking for truth and shouting out the answers you find.

EILA. You're a poet.

OZ *(looking into EILA's eyes).* I'm too poor to be a poet.

EILA. Poets are born with pencils in their teeth and paper on their tongues. You were born a poet. Help me build the bridge.

OZ. What bridge?

EILA. There are answers in here and out there in the great mystery that can change the way we live. The bridge to understanding has got to be sturdy. Are you strong?

OZ. I've mended the wings of butterflies.

EILA *(responds as if to OZ's touch).* You touched me. I remember you so clearly. If I close my eyes I can feel your breath on my neck, your hands on my spirit. I can see you so clearly. *(EILA in lighting effect is in an obvious trance state. It is not painful. Her voice, posture and focus are fluid with movement.)* Like a new penny heads up, like a bell in the distance, like love, I can see you like love in a pocketful of memories. *(Mimes.)* Blank eyes, dirty face, hands rattle three coins in a coffee cup. "Put some love in it. Put some love in it." *(End trance.)*

OZ. What's happening to you?

RUTH. She's going through the change. The ancestors are passing through her like a yellow-tailed sparrow. *(RUTH makes a swooping motion with her hand like a bird flying low, then claps.)* They were in my mother's hands, she could heal with the light in the palm of her right hand. When I started hearing clearly, she helped me through. She stayed here with me until Baybay started to see, then she opened her umbrella and was gone.

RUTH. The change is coming on Eila hard because Baybay is trying to leave. It's hard to do this work, let alone do it by yourself.

EILA. I see things. I feel things. I remember things in my bones. *(Walks around slightly confused as if she has been struck.)*

RUTH. I'll help you, much as I can. You never know when they're gonna pass through. *(Makes a swooping motion with her hand, then claps.)*

OZ. She's talking like she's somewhere else, somebody else. How did she see me?

RUTH. She's like a bowl of water under the bed. She's got the power to take things in. My family been listening to the ancestors too far back to mention. There comes a time when you have to make a choice to listen very carefully or you lose the gift. My daughter is sleeping and nothing ever comes to a sleeper but a dream.

(RUTH winks at OZ and waves him away. EILA picks up a book and refocuses. She hands him the book and a loaf of bread.)

EILA. Maybe you could come back tomorrow for breakfast. You get a free book every time. That's our specialty, books to nourish the soul. I'll make my special ink tea if you come, with literary soup and wisdom wine. I'll feed you.

RUTH. Go on, boy, you can go now.

EILA. The bridge has got to be built and it's got to be strong.

OZ. Butterflies.

EILA. There are roses under my cypresses.

OZ. In my dreams I suck at the breasts of light.

(OZ exits.)

(BAYBAY enters wearing a sexy dress and an elaborate hat.)

BAYBAY. Where's the flower boy? They let him go?

EILA. He danced for us, Mama. I think he might be the one.

RUTH *(wrinkling up her nose).* You smell like dead fish... And you look like a prostitute.

BAYBAY. I'm an artist and I can dress any way I want to.

EILA. Mama, you looking dangerous.

BAYBAY. It's a new look for my new life. I told you I'm selling this place and leaving these dusty memories behind.

RUTH. Always could find you looking in a mirror. Looking and masking.

BAYBAY. The long, blond, white girls get all the good parts. This brown Ginger is gonna dance with a copper-colored Fred. I'm gonna wake up in the promise land. Where all them promises come true. I've found somebody to love me.

RUTH. I spit on a West Indian woman once. Spit right in her face over some man I've long forgot. That woman cursed me. Told me I would soon have a burden to hain't me all my days. You were born right after that.

BAYBAY. Tell it to the ancestors.

RUTH. I know what love feels like. I was in love with a man that promised me the moon and the stars to string up in my own personal sky. Yes, I was in love once. Now I got me a relationship with the gods. Shango, Yemaya... That's what you need, granddaughter.

BAYBAY. She could be a nun, couldn't she? Is that what you mean? She could get engaged to God or even one of the Saints. We'll have a big wedding party and after that she can sit up in a musty old room with a crown of thorns on her head twisting a cheap wedding ring on her finger waiting to die and join the groom in heaven. Is that what you wanted for me, Mama? I got red honey between my thighs. I got sweet, mother's milk in my breasts. I've got desires.

(RUTH gets out of her chair, walks unsteadily over to BAYBAY leaning on her umbrella. RUTH shakes her hard then walks back to her chair and drops down in it wearily. BAYBAY stunned, stares at RUTH.)

RUTH. You don't talk to me like that. I am your mother like it or not. I won't tolerate disrespect from you or your child.

BAYBAY. You didn't earn it, Mama. You ruined my one chance at a little happiness. I will never forgive you for that, never. I came back here out of duty when you fell and broke your hip. You healed a long time ago, but I didn't. I release you, I release you, I release you.

(EILA watches them intently, frustrated as she has heard these arguments before.)

RUTH. You coulda had a lot more.

BAYBAY. I shoulda been on the cover of magazines. It shoulda been me receiving all them awards. I wrote a book. My future was set.

RUTH. Eila, give your mother a cool glass of water.

EILA. Mama, you and Grammie have always looked at two different sides of a three-headed coin. Let this rest.

BAYBAY. I was almost on the cover of a magazine. *(BAYBAY picks up a book, holds it to her chest and begins to recite.)* "The sun was crystal clear, looking in through the side of my head I could see him standing on the cliff just before he dived into the rocks graceful as a swan and his face shattered into a million stars and there was nothing left of him in it. He was dead and I was standing in the sun on the cliff laughing, still alive." I wrote that.

RUTH. You could hardly give away that mess you wrote back then, why you want to read it now?

(BAYBAY begins to cry.)

EILA. Grammie, you're being mean now.

BAYBAY. An important agent told me I had promise. He said my book could've been a Hollywood movie. He said it had potential.

RUTH. You were a gifted child, but you are hardheaded. You've got to feed people.

BAYBAY. I could do that with my art. You won't let me grow my wings. Eila! What's wrong with me? You must be starving. You want something to read?

EILA. We are supposed to be putting knowledge in the mouths and souls of the people who walk through that door. Marcus Garvey is here. Dorothy Dandridge is here. Malcolm X is here. Madam C.J. Walker is here. Sojourner Truth is here. We can't leave. Ain't I a woman, by any means necessary, back to Africa, hair miracles and star magic. *(Beat.)* Be wise, Mama. Be wise. You can teach me things. One and one makes *two...*

(BAYBAY joins EILA singing the childhood song, echoing her, and clapping hands like patty cake.)

BAYBAY. Honey, I love you...

EILA and BAYBAY. Two and two make four, Baby, where's the door? Three and three make six, Sugar, here's a good night kiss. Four and four make eight, Sandman, don't be late. Five and five make ten. Two four six eight ten, let's do it all over again.

BAYBAY. You remember that.

RUTH. You taught her that?

BAYBAY. Just like you taught it to me. Remember when I used to bathe you in the deep part of the kitchen sink, I'd sing that song to you...

RUTH. And blow bubbles in her face. She cried all the time. You never did know what to do for a baby.

BAYBAY. You taught me everything I know.
EILA. Will you two stop. I came home so I could...

RUTH. Bother us.

EILA. Mama...

BAYBAY. What's the matter, baby?

(As EILA speaks RUTH and BAYBAY repeat some of her words in a whisper, like an echo: Japanese, moans, sync, eyes.)

EILA. Loud music and voices and colors wake me up in the middle of the night. I went to see a madrina, a rootwoman, a healer, way up in Harlem. She burned blue incense, prayed over me and threw bones on the floor.

(Pause. EILA begins a trance. Her level of energy increases as she is taken over by the trance. It is not a painful experience, it is unexpected and out of her control. Lighting effect.)

EILA. I am walking down 42nd Street. Just walking, walking past the bright lights, the greasy smells, the loud colors. Car horns honking, leather-faced junkies trading dope in English, Spanish, and Japanese. *(Beat.)*

EILA. A woman screaming in the eye of an orgasm. There are homeless people stacked one on top of the
other. People in high-heeled shoes are dancing on top of their bodies. I am standing in the middle of a woman's stomach. I look right into her eyes. She is screaming. *(Yells out)* "Look into their eyes. Look into their eyes." *(End trance.)*

BAYBAY *(putting her arm around EILA)*. Ever since you was a little girl I told you that you were special, didn't I?

EILA. I understand that, but how...

BAYBAY. You've got to learn to walk with your feet on both sides of the street, baby.

EILA. Mama, does it happen to you like this?

BAYBAY. I've always heard them. When I was a baby they sounded like somebody was rolling the dial on the radio. By the time I could make out what they were saying Ididn't want to hear them. I didn't want to know all those things. It hurt.

RUTH. I saw them through my third eye. All colors, all kinds. The first ones looked like Africans. They walked right into my bedroom one night, sat on the floor around my bed and whispered to me all night long. After I got over the first shock we had right pleasant conversations. *(Beat.)* I'm a old woman, I need some rest. They been promising me a rest. Only thing left for me to do is get you settled and
open my umbrella. *(A car horn is heard.)*

BAYBAY. That must be Mr. Fine. My ticket to freedom. I ain't waiting around here no more. *(Snaps her fingers.)*

EILA. Mama, don't go. I need you.

BAYBAY. You'll be fine. She'll take care of you. I'll soon be sitting barefoot on my porch waiting for the sun to go down in front of my house. Mama, don't wait up for me.

(BAYBAY runs out the door.)

RUTH. They coming for me soon. That's why I got to get you settled. You'll be all right. I hated to see you go out into the world. I knew how much pain you was gonna have to take in before you come back.

EILA. They told me to come home. *(Trance with gestures.)* Home is where your heart can rest and your lips can suck at the breasts of love. A name, a train, a whisper in my soul.

RUTH. You were right to let them lead you. Just listen.

(Sound of many voices overlapping. Actors whisper lines from play. Lights fade out.)

SCENE TWO

SCENE: A sparse hotel room, one hour later.

AT RISE: *Lights fade up. Seduction music. BAYBAY and MR FINE are slow dancing.*

BAYBAY. Why did you choose me out of all the women in that club? Were you looking for me?

MR. FINE. I been looking for you all my life.

BAYBAY. How did you know it was me? Do you know them?

MR. FINE. Who?

BAYBAY. I been waiting for a long time. I just thought maybe they sent you.

MR. FINE. God is my witness, ain't nobody sent me but that sexy dress you was wearing called my name. Said, "Fine, come to mama." *(MR. FINE begins kissing her neck, caressing her face.)*

BAYBAY. I ain't felt like this in a long time. You sure they didn't send you?

MR. FINE. Woman, I told you ain't nobody sent me. The bartender told me you owned the store that give away books with breakfast.

BAYBAY *(pulls away from him).* So you did know who I was.

MR. FINE. I just wanted to check you out first, make sure you wasn't a professional or something.

BAYBAY. A professional what?!

MR. FINE. I didn't mean it like that. Look, let's just lay down on this nice soft bed, okay. Relax. Let me give you a massage.

BAYBAY. You sent me the most beautiful flowers. Do you love me?

MR. FINE. I've only known you for two days.

BAYBAY. Why you think I waited so long. *(MR. FINE kisses her.)* That's nice. Do you like the way I kiss?

MR. FINE. I'd like it better if you'd just relax. Lie down. The bed is nice and soft. Let's stop talking.

BAYBAY. Tell me about the club again. How many dance floors?

MR. FINE. I told you five times already.

BAYBAY. Tell me again. You make it sound so glamorous. It'll put me in the mood.

MR. FINE *(smooth).* I've been waiting for this opportunity. Every time I get a good deal going, something happens, somebody don't come through. You know, shit happens. But this time. This time it's gonna be different. I'm gonna be in charge. I'm gonna make all the decisions. Investors are gonna line up around the block. This is the set-up. VIPs only. Fine dining and dancing twenty-four hours a day for only the best people. People with class. I got friends, I know people. I'm not one to brag but I went to school with Mohammed Ali's cousin. I used to date Patti Labelle's sister's secretary. Patti's regular, good people. She'll come by if she's in town, sing a few songs. First thing I gotta do is decorate, bust down the walls and expand on the empty lot next to your place.

BAYBAY. The burial grounds are next door. Maybe the club could be on three levels.

MR. FINE. All them limos gotta have somewhere to park.

BAYBAY. But dead people are buried there, people who know us.

MR. FINE. Old bones are everywhere. Probably some under this hotel. This kinda hotel bound to have some bones in the closet too.

(BAYBAY jumps in her skin at the thought.)

BAYBAY *(stomping on the floor).* Are you sure? Where there are bones people are still there. *(Looks around the room.)*

MR. FINE. Nobody can see us. Come on over here. I want to get to know you.

BAYBAY. I want tonight to be perfect. Pinch me. I want to make sure this is real.

MR. FINE. You are one strange lady. *(He pinches her, begins to kiss her.)*

BAYBAY *(closes her eyes)*. Now promise me you'll never leave me. Promise me you'll always love me. Promise, promise me?

(Seduction music. Lights fade as they begin to make love.)

SCENE THREE

SCENE: *A street corner, the next day.*

AT RISE: *Lights up on OZ dancing, rhyming words and sounds accompanying himself by rattling a cup containing coins.*

OZ. Fine, wine, who got the line. Vote? Joke? Who got the rope. Sandman, black man hanging from a tree. Had no business trying to be free.

(MR. *FINE enters with a bunch of flowers. He tries to put a dollar in the cup but OZ evades him.)*

MR. FINE. I've got another delivery for you. Red tulips for the lady.

OZ. She's been waiting for you.

MR. FINE. I'm a master jazz man. I've been jazzing around for years, I know the score but I've never met a woman like her. There's something about this one. Something about her that's…different

OZ. Her mama's got talking bones. Her daughter tastes like daffodils. What does the lady taste like?

MR. FINE. Like a band of birds, like sweet success, like my chance at the end of the rainbow. I got a feeling my luck is about to change. That place and that woman just might turn my life around, in the direction my shoes are headed.

OZ. It's that kind of place. It sure has got a hold on me.

MR FINE. You about to get yourself into a situation you ain't in control of.

OZ. What do you mean?

MR. FINE. Let me give you some advice, son, it's the most valuable thing I could ever give you. Don't let nothing hold you back, not a woman, not a man and not a memory. The last thing my pop said to me was, "Son, don't listen to nothing that don't have a beat."

OZ. Maybe that was a sign. Maybe he wasn't talking about music. I'm listening to my heart and it's leading me back to that bookstore. I think that girl can see things I want to see.

MR. FINE. In your dreams.

OZ. Yea, in my dreams. I saw her in my dreams. That was my sign.

MR. FINE. I tried to get away like that once, but dreaming didn't hardly get me off Main Street. I don't have the patience to be waiting for signs and listening to voices like my folks did. The one time I got away from here I was gone for all of two weeks. All I wanted was for them to be proud of me. This time I'm taking the highway to fame and fortune, with the wind at my back and responsibility for nothing and nobody. The only signs I see now are dollar signs.

OZ. I'm taking the road that leads me home.

(OZ exits smelling the flowers. MR. FINE whistles a tune while flipping a coin into the air. He calls "Heads" then slaps the coin on the back of his hand.)

MR. FINE. Heads. Just like Mama said, "Call it like you want to see it."...

(Lights fade.)

SCENE FOUR

The bookstore, the next morning.

AT RISE: Lights up on EILA, preparing breakfast. She rips pages from a book and puts them into a pot of boiling water. She stirs and tastes her creation, adding a spice or two. Satisfied, she sits down at the table, checks her watch and stares at the door.

EILA. Five, four, three, two, one.

(On "one" OZ enters cautiously with the flowers.)

OZ. These are for the lady.

EILA. You're just in time for some nice hot soup.

OZ. What's in it?

EILA. The blood of Macbeth and leaves of grass. Tar babies and colored girls.

OZ. Blood and grass? You're joking, right?

EILA. When I was a little girl my mama put in a pinch of love with a short-handled spoon. Grammie's recipe was two cupped hands full of kindness. I add to that James Baldwin's fever, Maya Angelou's fire, Ntozake Shange's politics, Alice Walker's vision and Margaret Walker's never forget. I sprinkle words in the soup, words that bubble up to the top, then break into action. I stir in all the compassion I can find and a few tears and a few less fears. When I taste the soup I see things. I know things.

(EILA tastes the soup then trances.)

EILA
Two ears to the ground, four eyes closed, dreaming of someplace safe, someplace warm, someplace wanted. *(End trance.)* It hurts to look away.

OZ. *(He takes a sip of the soup.)* You want me to know things, don't you?

EILA. You already know things, I want you to bubble up and break into action.

(OZ breaks into a dance move.)

OZ. The old ladies here?

EILA. Grammie's still asleep. Mama didn't come home last night.

OZ. Are they okay being left alone? Did you come back to take care of them?

EILA. We take care of each other.

OZ. Are you like them?

EILA. What do you mean?

OZ. Do you hear voices too?

EILA. Sometimes. They guide me. Who do you listen to?

OZ. Can't say I be hearing things unless I haven't eaten for a few days. I guess I listen to myself, you know, deep inside. It's my feet got connections.

EILA. You've got some big feet.

OZ. Big feet run in my family.

EILA. What's your family like?

OZ. Mama was a healer, Daddy was a dreamer. They died in a plane crash a few years ago. My sister, Lois, told them not to leave that morning, begged them. She was the strange one in the family. My two brothers are both married. They live in the mid-west raising cows and corn and well-fed children.

EILA. Where's your sister?

OZ. After my folks died, she was depressed for a long time. She's in Blackstone now.

EILA. Where's that?

OZ. The cemetery.

EILA. Do you talk to her?

OZ. I just told you, she's dead.

EILA. I talk to dead people all the time. They can hear you.

OZ. In the cemetery....six feet underground.

EILA. When you're alone, when you miss her most, call out her name.

(EILA lights a candle and pours water in a bowl on an altar with photos of deceased relatives.)

EILA
I offer you coolness and light. *(Calls out each name three times.)* Nettie Mae...Zaliotis...Mary Lee...Moses...Carrie Bessie...Lillian... Luellen...Charlie Mae...(*Trance*) There's no heaven, no sky in empty bowls. Hell freezes bare feet and scorches the bones of misery. Look into their eyes!

(RUTH has entered, witnessed EILA's trance.)

RUTH. She's standing in the eye of the storm. She's strong, she'll make it with your help.

OZ. What am I supposed to do?

RUTH. Stay a while, you got a hungry smell. You can feed each other.

OZ. I need something...

RUTH. I know. She needs something too. Do you think you could love her? I'm talking about genuine love.

OZ. Do raindrops fall?

RUTH. Now that's a proper question. Eila, you think you could love him?

EILA. Is my soul is on fire.

RUTH. You'll need a good friend and a strong love for what's ahead. It's almost time for me to raise my umbrella. You'll soon be on your own.

EILA. How do you know when it's time, Grammie?

RUTH. It's in the bones. Besides, my batteries are getting weak, the reception ain't as clear as it used to be. Everything and everybody gets used up over time. I'm tired and I just want to rest and dance that final cakewalk. *(RUTH does a dance step.)* You two go on down to the park and eat some flowers or something. When your mama comes home I need to have a talk with her.

EILA. Be nice.

RUTH *(mocking her).* Be nice. I'm her mother, I don't have to be no ways nice. Go on now.

OZ. I got good intentions.

RUTH. That's a start. You got a big heart too. Hers is big as a Buick.

(EILA and OZ exit. RUTH throws the bones, listens then begins a conversation.)

RUTH. A heart as big as the Chrysler Building and hanging off her sleeve...(Pause.) One time I had a heart that big and a love that wide. I didn't think I could love Boston and listen to y'all too. When Boston was courting me he brought me flowers and a cat. I thought that was sweet, I let him come live with us.

RUTH. I thought he was a good man. And then there was the night I come home and found him in my bed with my baby. There was blood on her thighs. What was a mother to do? I would shoot that rotten, low-life piece of trash and bury him in the backyard ten more times. 'Course she don't remember nothing before she woke up in the hospital holding the most beautiful baby I ever saw. For nine months she lived in a dream. She's still dreaming. Why you give her such a long dream?

(RUTH is stirring and tasting the soup. BAYBAY enters, her clothes are in disarray. The women exchange glances. BAYBAY drops her eyes first.)

BAYBAY. I'm grown, Mama.

RUTH. You're still my child.

BAYBAY. Is it wrong to want somebody to love me?

RUTH. What about me and Eila? We can't live like everybody else. We got responsibilities here.

BAYBAY. I need arms to wrap around my soul, kisses to go deeper than that. I think they sent Mr. Fine, Mama. And maybe they sent that flower boy for Eila.

RUTH. They said there would be a sign. Strangers coming.

BAYBAY. I been looking at symbols and I been looking in the mirror for any sign of change. I been waiting for something to shake me inside of my skin.

RUTH. You ought to be thinking about your daughter. She needs you to help her.

BAYBAY. Like you helped me. You killed my opportunity.

RUTH. Baybay, stop lying to yourself. Boston took advantage of you.

BAYBAY. He said I was beautiful. He said my prose was beautiful. He promised he would take me away to someplace beautiful. I needed somebody to tell me all of that. It hurt not to know. He promised me things.

RUTH. He hurt you, baby.

BAYBAY. You hurt me Mama. You hurt me.

RUTH. I was protecting you.

BAYBAY. You lie, you lie, you lie.

RUTH. You needed me.

BAYBAY. I needed you to tell me how beautiful I was, how smart and funny. I am every ounce of me because of you. It was some kind of love I had, and you couldn't stand that. You couldn't stand me having a life of my own. It meant leaving you here alone with the ancestors. You're the one who's scared. You need me, Mama. You need me!

(BAYBAY exits. Sound of Ancestors many voices whispering, overlapping. Lights fade.)

SCENE FIVE

SCENE: *MR FINE'S car, the next day.*

AT RISE: Lights up. *Upbeat jazz music plays on the car radio, sunny, carefree kind of music. MR. FINE and BAYBAY both wear hats and dark glasses. As MR FINE drives his white Lincoln Continental down the street, they hum along improvising loudly.*

MR. FINE. You look so sweet, baby, you make my teeth hurt.

BAYBAY. Talk that talk.

MR. FINE. I'm just telling the truth. Why you think I been sending you flowers everyday? You're like honey to a bee.

BAYBAY. Them flowers you been sending make that musty old bookstore smell like the Garden of Eden.

MR. FINE. Once we get started on the renovations you gonna think you living hi the Garden of Eden. That place is gonna spank and sparkle, bloom in every season. We'll fly in wild orchids from Colombia, palm trees from Florida. Paradise baby. You like that? We gonna be living the good life, the high life. Yeah, lola Fine's little dreamer is about to wake up in the big time. Got myself a good woman, a good idea and all I got to do is keep moving in the passing lane.

(He swerves the car and she crashes into him.)

BAYBAY. I've got a confession to make. I'm a little scared.

MR. FINE. What you scared of? I been driving since I could walk. I could've raced cars if I'd wanted to.

BAYBAY. I'm not scared of your driving. I'm scared of leaving. I mean letting go of that place. Every time I try to get away from them they seem to drag me back. One time I woke up in a hotel in New Orleans and I felt one of 'em standing at the foot of my bed pulling on my big toe. Nothing changes in that place but the weather and the numbers on the calendar. Love can change things.

MR. FINE. Your life will never be the same with me. Baby, I know five kinds of karate and used to be on the wrestling team when I was in school. Woman, I'd wrestle alligators for you. Why I'd bite the head off a rattlesnake for you. Now if that's not love, what is?

BAYBAY. Every morning I wake up in your arms I see angels flapping their jealous wings around your head. I'm just too happy for it to last.

MR. FINE. You see angels? *(Movie music begins to swell)*

BAYBAY. Angels. *(Flaps her wings.)* You can see things too. Look! Look there between the rhythm. Don't you see the sound? Listen to the symbols. There, that's a sign.

MR. FINE. What do the signs say?

BAYBAY. Sharp curves. Paradise ahead. *(Lights fade.)*

INTERMISSION

SCENE SIX

The bookstore, the next day.

AT RISE: *EILA unpacks a box of books calling out the titles and number of copies. BAYBAY is removing books from the shelves, stacking them like building blocks, ignoring EILA.)*

EILA. *Africanisms in American Culture* edited by Joseph E. Hollaway, three. *Before the Mayflower: A History of Black America* by Lerone Bennett Jr., three. *The Mis-Education of the Negro* by Carter G. Woodson, three. *Vibration Cooking* by Verta Mae Grosvenor, three. *How Europe Underdeveloped Africa* by Walter Rodney, three. *Women, Race and Class* by Angela Davis, two. *Beloved* by Toni Morrison, three.

(Notices BAYBAY stacking the books.)

EILA. Mama, what are you doing?

BAYBAY. It don't make a teaspoon full of sense for you to be doing inventory. We'll be closing soon.

EILA. We ain't going nowhere. Grammie said she got to pass on the bones and the stories got to be sipped like wine.

BAYBAY. I'm gonna be drinking champagne from now on. I'm gonna wear wild Colombian orchids in my hair. I'm moving on.

EILA. You always leaving me when I need you the most.

BAYBAY. What are you talking about?

EILA. I would close my eyes at night and see you on a highway in a foreign car the color of the moon. A fast car with the top down, you holding on to one of your ridiculous hats, laughing with some man driving you into the stars. I would search every constellation for your shiny blue dress or your flowered hat. I would listen for the sound of your voice approaching, the click of your high-heel shoes on the hardwood floor of my bedroom coming to kiss me goodnight. I wished and I waited. Me and Grammie always ended up taking care of your world wounds.

BAYBAY *(surprised)*. The stars were further away than I imagined. I just wanted to make a tiny hole out there, big enough for the three of us to slip through unnoticed.

EILA. Why didn't you take me with you?

BAYBAY. Ruth wouldn't let me take you to the corner for an ice cream cone.

EILA. I was your child.

BAYBAY. No, you were hers from the moment you were born. I mean she took you from me. I was dreaming the most beautiful dream. I was flying through rooms and windows, through other countries and other worlds. I experienced a lifetime, no time, time moved quickly and stood still. When I came back you belonged to her. I was crying on the inside.

EILA. Your leaving hurt me.

BAYBAY. You reminded me of the most hurtful thing that ever happened to me. I couldn't dream or fly when you were around. You kept me too close to the ground with my ears and eyes too open. I didn't mean to hurt you, baby, I just needed to dream.

EILA. I need you. Please be my mama. Let me lean on you this time. Please.

BAYBAY. I don't know how.

(BAYBAY looks at her silently then exits. Lights fade.)

SCENE SEVEN

The bookstore, two weeks later. There are bunches of dead flowers all around the stage.

AT RISE: *RUTH is ripping newspaper into strips. EILA is sitting on the sofa reading a book.*

RUTH. You got sense enough to use protection? You do understand the consequences of social intercourse, don't you?

EILA. What do you mean?

RUTH. You got to protect yourself, baby. You're like a little sponge trying to sop up the sea.

EILA. What am I supposed to do? People are hungry out there. I can feed them.

(RUTH taps her hearing aid to better hear the voices.)

RUTH. What? What you say? Fever? Oh, feed. Baby, you can feed them one by one, a day at a time. *(Sings.)* "When you get tired and weary turn to the one you love. When your hands are full and wet with tears turn to the one you love, to the one you love." Being here in this place is a blessing and a curse but it's our reason for living.

EILA. When Mama used to leave us to go off looking around out there, I would forget about her until she showed up with a new hat and a heart full of disappointments. I used to wonder if she was really my mama. She was a like a tourist from a foreign country. She even spoke another language.

RUTH. She always came back.

EILA. You made it safe here, you made it all seem so ordinary, living with the bones. You been preparing me for this, haven't you?

RUTH. Both of you.

EILA. She's talking about leaving again.

RUTH. That's just talk. Your mother is chasing her last rainbow.

(BAYBAY enters. BAYBAY's music.)

BAYBAY. And I'm gonna catch one. I can feel beautiful things out there. I'm a different person. *(Reading from a notebook.)* "We kissed a whole season. I surrendered. We were swimming on the horizon. I felt a hurricane coming, we were pulled by the undertow, split open, devoured, licked clean. After the storm the most exquisite calm. Our flesh parted in dreams. We woke up the dawn clinging to each other." I wrote that. *(To RUTH.)* Last night I saw things I've never seen before. *(RUTH begins to clang pans together to drown out BAYBAY.)* Mr. Fine loves me. He promised me a real life out there.

EILA. When do we get to meet this Mr. Fine?

BAYBAY. Soon enough. Where's the messenger boy?

EILA. (picks up a bowl) I fed his soul. *(Trance.EILA's music.)* When I step off the train I feel the suffering. I see hunger and broken people. They ask me for money. I empty my pockets. I eat in restaurants with white linen on the tables, I see hungry minds in the window. I put leftovers from the Chinese restaurant on top of a garbage can and leave a pair of clean chopsticks and a napkin for the woman wearing a blue blanket tied with rope. She is chewing on bread she peels from cracks in the sidewalk. I take off my shoes and walk up to women and men I don't know and I kiss them on the lips in broad daylight. I kiss a woman with holes in her shoes. I kiss her on the mouth. I kiss a man missing teeth and the third finger of his left hand. A man is lying on the steps of a church. A policeman comes to wake him up and move him on. The man says that he has nowhere to go and wants to go to jail. The policeman tells the man that he can't take him to jail unless he commits a crime. The man says, "What crime do I have to commit to be given some food to eat? I'm cold and tired." The policeman says any crime will do. When the policeman turns his back the man throws a rock and breaks a stained glass window in the church.

(End trance.)

EILA. His bowl is empty I feed him pieces of my heart. He grows strong and begins to build a nation. I touch things, I can see. What now? What am I supposed to do now?

RUTH. Now you can read the bones.

(RUTH taps on her hearing aid. MR. FINE knocks, then enters with a large bunch of flowers.)

MR. FINE. Good evening, pretty ladies.

RUTH. Ain't no pretty ladies in here. We all women in here. Baybay, look at what he got in his hands. Some more of them flowers.

(BAYBAY rushes over to take the flowers. MR. FINE kisses her hand.)

BAYBAY. Good evening, Mr. Fine. You are such a gentleman.

MR. FINE. Is this your lovely daughter?

RUTH. Take your eyes off my granddaughter. Baybay, will you stop all this foolishness.

BAYBAY. Mama, it's not foolishness.

RUTH. Our blood and bones have nourished this soil for longer than memory.

BAYBAY. Nobody comes here anymore.

RUTH. That doesn't mean we can just leave. The Creator blew breath into a handful of dust. Made the miracle of woman and man. The spirits of the first people are here. Our voices. The sound is clear and strong in this place. They ain't going nowhere and neither am I. Neither are you.

MR. FINE. Ma'am, your daughter and I have plans for our future.

RUTH. You can't pave over bones.

BAYBAY. I'm not happy here.

BAYBAY *(goes to kneel by RUTH, pleading).* Mama, don't spoil my second

RUTH. You wouldn't be happy in heaven. Who needs happiness all the time? Every minute of my life wasn't jump up and joy. I'd have died a long time ago if I was waiting on happy.

MR. FINE. Are you sure you want to do this?

BAYBAY. I want to make a new start with you. *(Beat.)* I'm forgetting my manners. I invited you to dinner and here I am running off at the mouth.

RUTH. I ain't eating with no stranger trying to take my daughter and run me outta my own place.

BAYBAY. Mama, I'm not gonna stand for you being rude. Me and Mr. Fine have got a dream and you can't drown it. We don't need your permission to make it happen. We don't even need this place, we can make it anywhere.

MR.FINE. But baby, I got big plans.

RUTH. Hissss. Hissss. Hissss. You ain't nothing but a two-legged snake. This is my place and will be even after I'm dead. You wanna take a chance I won't hain't you?

MR. FINE. I'm willing to take that chance since I don't believe in ghosts or spirits. Baybay, I'm gonna take care of everything.

BAYBAY. Are you gonna take care of me?

RUTH. Baybay, think about what you doing. I don't have long. Let me leave this world knowing I still have my place.

EILA. Every time you leave here you come back with bigger dreams.

BAYBAY. Who needs this old, broken-down place. We could open a club in New York, L.A. or Paris. Let me get my hat, we can leave right now. There ain't nothing holding me back.

MR. FINE. Hold up, baby, it's gonna take a little time. I've got to build my reputation.

BAYBAY. You can build a nightclub anywhere.

MR. FINE. Sweetheart, this is my town. I told you, I got friends here, I know people. I'm just getting my career started. I can't leave now. Aretha's got a concert at the Civic Center next month.

RUTH *(sarcastic and unbelieving).* Aretha.

BAYBAY. You know Aretha Franklin?

MR. FINE. Know her, we grew up in the same neighborhood. (Beat) I figure it like this: Aretha could make aguest appearance for the grand opening at Mr. Fine's Hideaway. Fine dining, dancing and entertainment twenty-four hours a day, just like I said.

BAYBAY. Are you sure? You talking about R-E-S-P-E-C-T , Find out what it means to me- Spanish Harlem-Chain of Fools-Amazing Grace-Natural Woman-Pink Cadillac-Aretha Franklin?

MR. FINE. The one. Tina Turner's coming for Christmas and Smokey Robinson just might bring the Miracles back together in time for Valentine's Day. I'm telling you we got to move on this now. I got a call from the architect this morning. The blueprints are ready. All we got to do is sign a few papers, get a few more investors and BAM. BOOM. We gonna be making history and enough money to go all them places you want to go. I got it all planned.

RUTH. You gonna have to carry out those plans somewhere else. Tell that man we can't leave, baby.

BAYBAY. Mama, please. (No answer.) Don't kill this happiness too.

RUTH. I'm trying to save you from another heartache.

BAYBAY. You lie.

RUTH. He hurt you.

BAYBAY. You lie.

RUTH. I'm sorry I let him hurt you.

BAYBAY. You lie. You don't think I can do it, do you? I'll show you all of you. (Snaps her fingers.) I'm outta here.

(Voices of the ancestors overlap.)

MR. FINE. I'm with you, baby. Everything's gonna work out fine.

(BAYBAY and FINE exit. Lights fade.)

SCENE EIGHT

*AT RISE: MR.FINE is driving the car as BAYBAY looks out the
window to see if they are being followed.*

MR. FINE. Where are we going?

BAYBAY. Just drive until I forget my old address.

MR. FINE. How about some music?

BAYBAY. Wrap me up in something warm and mellow.

(FINE turns on the radio. He rolls the dial until he comes to some
sentimental jazz. They hum along, laughing.)

BAYBAY. Tell me a story, about when you were a little boy.

MR. FINE. I can't remember that far back.

BAYBAY. C'mon, you must remember something. What do little
boys do with their daddies?

MR. FINE. (pauses, looks at her to see if he can be vulnerable with
her.) One time my daddy took me hunting. I was about seven or
eight years old. We walked through the woods for a long time
without seeing anything but tree branches and grey sky. We walked
until we came to an old dead tree lying across the road. Just as we
were getting ready to step over it, a long, black snake crawled out
and lay there looking at us. For a long time Daddy didn't move and I
was too scared to breathe. After a while, Daddy said, "Guess we
won't be hunting in these woods today." When he said that, the
snake seemed to hear him. It went on its way and we went on ours.

BAYBAY. I wonder which spirit it was?

MR. FINE. We never went hunting for sport again. Daddy talked a
lot, even when no one seemed to be around. People thought he
was crazy. I left here to get away from all that. I haven't been back
to those little-boy memories since.

BAYBAY. I'm sorry.

MR. FINE. Wasn't your fault. I wonder if it just wasn't the right time to leave. What about you, when you were a little girl?

BAYBAY. When I was a little girl, my mother used to love me. When I was about thirteen years old, Mama was combing my hair out on the back porch just before sunset. Suddenly a flock of birds landed on an old dead tree in front of us. They were the most beautiful birds, with red wings and bright yellow eyes. I was stunned. Then Mama started singing to them and they seemed to be talking back to her in a language I couldn't understand. All of a sudden the birds seemed to disappear inside the tree, and I could still see them. They started talking to me and I could understand them. (Beat) Look, we're coming to the city. I can see the lights.

MR. FINE. Is that snow?

BAYBAY. It looks like…they're leaves.

MR. FINE. Yellow…

BAYBAY. …leaves.

MR. FINE. (stops the car on a dime) There's a tree growing in the middle of the road.

MANY VOICES (*sing, voiceover*) I am an old, old soul. I have been here a very long time. I am the beginning of all things. I am the end of the road. You've come to the middle of your journey, yet you have a long way to go. This is your destiny: Home. Listen to the talking bones.

BAYBAY. We have to go back.

(*Lights fade.*)

SCENE NINE

AT RISE: Lights come up as OZ and EILA step out the door of the bookstore holding hands. They seem to be walking but not getting anywhere, as if on a treadmill.

OZ. Do you really think we can find them?

EILA. We can try.

OZ. What if we can't.

EILA. We can't think like that or it won't work. Just keep moving forward and hold on to my hand.

OZ. My feet hurt.

EILA. Mine too.

OZ. Is that snow? No, it looks like leaves.

EILA. Yellow leaves.

OZ. Look, there's something in the road. It's a tree growing in the middle of the road.

(Snatch of the song, whispered voices are heard.)

EILA. We need to go back.

(They turn around to face the bookstore. EILA starts toward the door. Lights fade.

SCENE TEN

AT RISE: Lights come up on RUTH and EILA, who is stirring the pot of soup. BAYBAY and MR. FINE enter.

RUTH: What you come back for?

BAYBAY: Let him taste the soup.

RUTH. What?

BAYBAY. The soup. Let him taste it.

RUTH. Is he ready?

EILA. Does he want to?

MR. FINE. I sure could use a bowl of something hot. I'm hungry as a hole in the road.

RUTH. (to BAYBAY) Are you ready?

BAYBAY. Mama, will you comb my hair?

(BAYBAY holds out a comb to RUTH; she takes it. BAYBAY sits beside her on the floor. Just as RUTH touches her head, she speaks.)

BAYBAY. I've always wanted to fly. Just flap my wings and take off into sky blue. Straight up and then out over the land, dipping into the clouds until everything below me is small and insignificant. Just the sound of the wind. I would live in the trees. I've only been able to do that in my dreams.

RUTH. When did you start dreaming about flying?

BAYBAY. When Boston hurt me.

RUTH. I'm so sorry baby.

BAYBAY. Boston took away all my pretty, my soft and sweet. When he hurt me I seemed to fly above my body, out of the window and into some other worlds. They saved me from flying out of the window when I was awake.

RUTH. When he hurt you I heard the most ferocious roar in my ears. I found the strength of a thousand mothers in my arm. (Beat.) Can you forgive me?

BAYBAY. I'll wrap you in my wings, Mother Dear.

EILA. Let's give him a taste.

RUTH. Is he strong enough?

BAYBAY. I've got to find out.

(BAYBAY offers MR. FINE a sip of soup. He tastes, smiles approvingly then helps himself to a bowl which he eats throughout the scene.)

RUTH. When I was a little girl I used to dream about them. Tall, pipe-smoking medicine men and healing women wrapped in blankets. Sometimes I be sleeping in my bed and they'd come to me four, five, six of 'em all talking at once. I love listening to souls speak.

EILA. Mama said they were speaking in tongues the night I was born.

RUTH. It snowed that night. Look like it's gonna snow tonight.

MR. FINE. I'm afraid we're not in a position to get snow. It would be something of a miracle for that to happen.

RUTH. You a weatherman?

BAYBAY. Last time it snowed round here, they helped me make Eila.

MR. FINE. How did they do that?

BAYBAY. How do you think I got her?

MR. FINE. How women always get them. *(Sings, unaware he is affected by the soup.)* "When a man loves a woman..." *(MR. FINE hums or sings low through BAYBAY's story.)*

BAYBAY. Eila was made in the desert on an island under a blanket of stars and snow. They were chanting and beating drums. They said, "Open your eyes. Open your eyes." They drew me to them and snow began to fall all around us. When I woke up, I knew Eila was with me, growing inside of me.

RUTH. She and the messenger are building the bridge.

(OZ's music.)

MR. FINE. Did you hear that? What's that sound?

(OZ enters holding a bowl made from newspaper. It is filled with large, red, heart-shapes.)

OZ. The sky is so tender tonight. I brought something for you.

MR. FINE. What is it?

OZ. A bowl of homemade love.

(OZ gives a heart to each of them.)

MR. FINE. I'll never forget the first time I saw you. You was dancing that crazy dance of yours. You had a cup in your hands, you were talking about... put some love in it.

OZ. You tried to put money in it.

MR. FINE. With enough money...

EILA. You can't buy love.

OZ. You can give it away.

MR. FINE. You think my life's been easy chasing one dream after the other? Just once I want to come across the finish line first. Get the pretty girl, drive the fast car and take it to the bank. BAM. Iola and Pretty Fine's little dreamer finally made it. (*He perks as if hearing someone he can't see.*)

RUTH. Eila! Oz. (*RUTH points to one of the altars. EILA and OZ begins lighting candles at each altar, saying a prayer.*) Feed him some soup.

EILA. I offer you love and thanks. (*She lights a candle.*)

OZ. I offer you coolness and refreshment. (Pours water.)

EILA. I offer you light and energy.

OZ. Please help us find the way.

RUTH. What you gonna do now, Mr. Fine?

MR. FINE. What does a ten-year old boy know about taking care of a family? One mistake led to another because I didn't have a map. I kept getting lost.

RUTH. What you gonna do now, Mr. Fine? (*Beat*) Baybay, give him your heart.

MR. FINE. As long as you drew breath, you believed in me, Mama.

RUTH. Say their names, Mr. Fine.

MR. FINE. Iola and Pretty Fine? Iola and Pretty Fine? Iola and Pretty Fine?

(*Ancestor voices grow stronger and slightly more recognizable.*)

VOICES. Arthur? Arthur?

MR. FINE. Mom? Pop?

VOICES. Life is a along shot and you been betting on losers. You can win. You keep looking outside and it's in you. It's here. It's in you. It's here. It's in you.

MR. FINE. Hey I heard it. It's in me? (Beat) I heard it. It's in me. I heard it.

BAYBAY. You can hear them? You can hear them! He can hear them. (*to FINE*) Do you believe me now? (*Starts to dance*)

MR. FINE. What was in that soup?

EILA. Lion hearts and rose petals. Wings of desire and the mockingbird's song.

OZ. Homemade love.

MR. FINE. Baybay, I heard…I heard the future.

RUTH. Now what you gonna do, Mr. Fine?

MR. FINE. We'll knock out that wall and build a bigger kitchen. And… and we'll make a loft over there where Baybay can write some more books.

BAYBAY. (ecstatic) I know just how the new book will start: "In 1959, Ruth, mother of Baybay, grandmother of Eila, opened Ancestor's Books and Breakfast with thirteen copies of The History of Our Spirits, The History of Ourselves and a bottomless pot of literary soup. And when souls came seeking, they sipped the stories with wisdom wine. Like life, the stories do not end. They never end.

RUTH. Plant my tree so the roots will lead me home.

BAYBAY *(to RUTH).* I'll be calling your name.

(RUTH throws the bones center stage and circles them clockwise. The voices whisper. RUTH opens her umbrella with a flourish and glittery confetti splashes over this scene. RUTH begins to dance a spirited cakewalk. BAYBAY puts her hand to her mouth in surprise, acceptance, then letting go. MR. FINE looks on as OZ, EILA and BAYBAY shuffle a joyous, New Orleans-style funeral march around RUTH. As RUTH dances offstage a visual image of her is projected onto the umbrella. In the projection, she is dancing through an old cemetery waving a bouquet of white carnations. Sound of the ancestors' loud, whispering, voices overlapping, joyous, hopeful. BAYBAY begins to dig a hole, OZ brings the water, EILA brings earth, FINE has the tree which they plant for RUTH.)

END

Made in the USA
Monee, IL
15 July 2025

21204273R00038